TOP TENS

ANCIENT BEASTS

ticktock

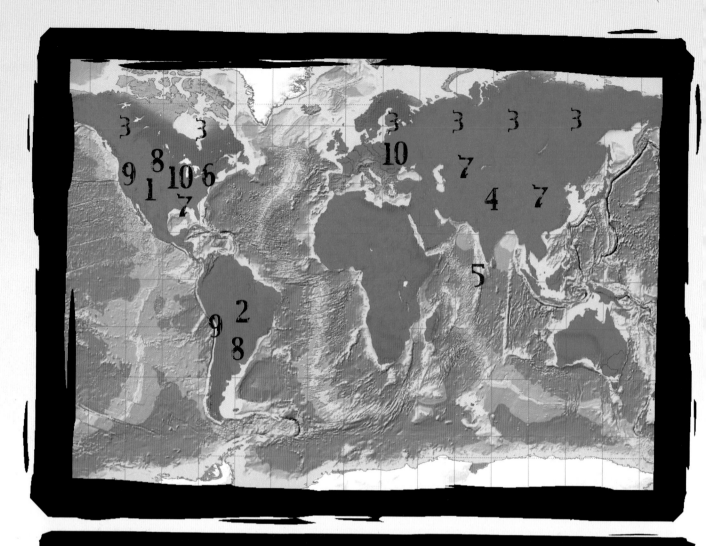

1 ENTELODON
2 PHORUSRHACOS
3 MAMMOTHS
4 INDRICOTERES
5 AMBULOCETUS
6 CHALICOTHERES
7 ANDREWSARCHUS
8 SABRE TOOTHED CATS
9 MACRAUCHENIA
10 GASTORNIS

Copyright © ticktock Entertainment Ltd 2005
First published in Great Britain in 2005 by ticktock Media Ltd,
Unit 2, Orchard Business Centre, North Farm Road, Tunbridge Wells, Kent TN2 3XF
ISBN 1 86007 910 5 pbk
Printed in China
A CIP catalogue record for this book is available from the British Library.

Picture credits (t=top; b=bottom; c=centre; l=left; r=right): Bookmatrix: 6-7 all, 8-9 all, 24-25 all, 18-19 all, 22-23 all. Natural History Museum: 2b, 4-5 all, 10-11 all, 12-13 all, 14-15 all. Luis Rey: 16-17 all. Pulsar: 20-21 all. Simon Mendez: 26-27 all.

We would be pleased to insert the appropriate acknowledgements in any subsequent edition of this publication.

CONTENTS

This book is a catalogue of the most impressive of the ancient beasts that lived after the dinosaurs were wiped out some 65 million years ago. The sudden disappearance of the dinosaurs created numerous opportunities for the birds and mammals that survived the collision. Some of them grew larger, stronger, and fiercer than any mammals or birds before or since. We have rated these ancient beasts according to:

FIGHTING SKILLS

All animals are either predators or prey, and they all need effective fighting skills in order to survive. Predators obviously scored highly here, but we also found some herbivores capable of putting up a ferocious defence. Points were awarded for teeth, tusks, claws, and potential kicking power.

NO.9   MACRAUCHENIA

Macrauchenia was a very strange, long-necked mammal that had a short, muscular trunk. It lived in South America, where it fed on leaves and other kinds of plant food. The famous scientist Charles Darwin discovered the first fossils of Macrauchenia in the 1830s during his voyage around the world on the ship *Beagle*.

BODY MASS
Apart from the strange trunk, Macrauchenia looked rather like a camel, but without the hump. Its front legs were about 3 metres long. Its name means long term.

SKULL SIZE
Its skull was fairly small. The strange arrangement of the openings in the skull — the nostrils are located between the eyes — enabled scientists to work out that Macrauchenia had an elephant-like trunk.

FIGHTING SKILLS
This plant-eating mammal was not equipped for a fight — it had no horns, **tusks**, claws or sharp teeth. Its only hope was to run faster than the **predators**.

8

BODY MASS

In this category we gave the most points to animals with the greatest weight. In cases where there is not enough fossil evidence for an accurate estimate of an animal's weight, we took note of its height or length instead.

SKULL SIZE

Skull size tends to be a good indicator of an animal's comparative success, and we awarded points accordingly. A large skull usually means large jaws or a large beak, which allows the animal to feed more efficiently. A larger skull also provides room for larger eyes; and it may also accommodate a larger brain, although this is by no means always the case.

SPEED

Both predators and prey benefit from being able to move quickly, but speed alone is not everything. There is no point in being able to run (or swim) faster than your prey, if you cannot change direction easily, or come to a sudden stop. Our ancient beasts were given points for their speed, acceleration, and overall agility.

EXISTED FOR

All the animals in this book are extinct — they died out at some time in the past. We gave points according to how long ago these ancient beasts lived, the estimated longevity of individuals, and the length of time that the species survived. Extra points were given to those animals that lived in extreme conditions (e.g. during the Ice Age).

Despite its ungainly appearance, Macrauchenia was a fast and agile runner.

SPEED

The arrangements of the bones and **joints** in the lower part of the legs indicate to scientists that Macrauchenia was able to change direction at high-speed when being chased by a predator.

EXISTED FOR

It lived mainly during the **Pliocene** period, but only became extinct about 20,000 years ago.

The reconstructed skeleton of Macrauchenia illustrate a stooped stance.

EXTREME SCORES

It might not mean you any harm, but Macrauchenia could kick you out of the way without even noticing you.

= TOTAL SCORE

GASTORNIS

Gastornis was a large, flightless bird that lived not long after the land-living dinosaurs died out. It lived in the forests of Europe, where it may have hunted small **mammals,** using its huge beak to seize its **prey.** French scientist Gaston Planté discovered **fossils** of Gastornis in 1855 near Paris, France.

SKULL SIZE

The back half of the skull was fairly normal, but the front half, with the huge beak, was enormous. The beak itself was three times bigger than the rest of the skull put together.

Gastornis raided the nests of mammals and other birds.

FIGHTING SKILLS

Scientists cannot decide whether Gastornis was a plant-eater that used its beak for cracking nuts; or a **carnivore** that used its beak to rip open its prey. If attacked, Gastornis would have kicked out with the sharp claws on its feet.

SPEED

Gastornis had small, stumpy wings and could not fly. It had little use for high-speed movement because it lived in thick forests where running was difficult.

BODY MASS

Gastornis stood about 1.75 metres tall. Although it was shorter than a present-day ostrich, it was more heavily built.

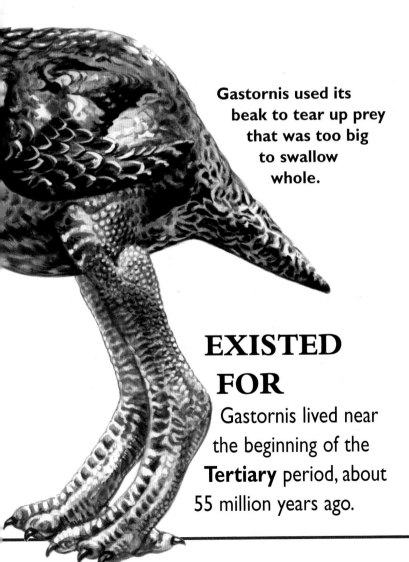

Gastornis used its beak to tear up prey that was too big to swallow whole.

EXISTED FOR

Gastornis lived near the beginning of the **Tertiary** period, about 55 million years ago.

A big bird with a massive beak and a taste for the flesh of mammals – it would not make a nice pet.

BODY MASS
3/10

SKULL SIZE
5/10

FIGHTING SKILLS
6/10

SPEED
6/10

EXISTED FOR
6/10

= TOTAL SCORE

MACRAUCHENIA

Macrauchenia was a very strange, long-necked **mammal** that had a short, muscular trunk. It lived in South America, where it fed on leaves and other kinds of plant food. The famous scientist Charles Darwin discovered the first **fossils** of Macrauchenia in the 1830s during his voyage around the world on the ship *Beagle*.

BODY MASS

Apart from the strange trunk, Macrauchenia looked rather like a camel, but without the hump. Its front legs were about 3 metres long. Its name means "long llama".

SKULL SIZE

Its skull was fairly small. The strange arrangement of the openings in the skull – the nostrils are located between the eyes – enabled scientists to work out that Macrauchenia had an elephant-like trunk.

FIGHTING SKILLS

This plant-eating mammal was not equipped for a fight – it had no horns, **tusks**, claws or sharp teeth. Its only hope was to run faster than the **predators**.

Despite its ungainly appearance, Macrauchenia was a fast and agile runner.

SPEED

The arrangements of the bones and **joints** in the lower part of the legs indicate to scientists that Macrauchenia was able to change direction at high-speed when being chased by a predator.

EXISTED FOR

It lived mainly during the **Pliocene** period, but only became extinct about 20,000 years ago.

The reconstructed skeleton of Macrauchenia illustrate a stooped stance.

It might not mean you any harm, but Macrauchenia could kick you out of the way without even noticing you.

BODY MASS
8/10

SKULL SIZE
4/10

FIGHTING SKILLS
2/10

SPEED
8/10

EXISTED FOR
5/10

= TOTAL SCORE
27/50

Sabre-toothed cats were fierce and deadly **ice-age carnivores**. Species such as *Smilodon* in North America and *Homotherium* in Africa were the top **predators** of all they surveyed. Some of the finest sabre-toothed **fossils** are those of Smilodon that were discovered in the La Brea tar pits in California, USA.

BODY MASS

These beasts were about the same size as present-day big cats, and weighed about 200 kilograms.

Sabre-toothed cats used their teeth to attack the soft belly of their prey.

SKULL SIZE

A sabre-toothed cat had a skull about 30 centimetres long, with two canine teeth projecting down from the front of its upper **jaw**.

FIGHTING SKILLS

Sabre-toothed cats were ambush hunters. These cats probably used their long teeth for slashing at the vulnerable undersides of their **prey**.

The other teeth are tiny in comparison to the two "sabres".

SPEED

They had shorter legs than other big cats, and were not designed for speed. They could only run over very short distances.

EXISTED FOR

The sabre-toothed cats lived during the **Pliocene** epoch.

A ferocious hunter with the longest cutting teeth of any **mammal**, this was not a cute little kitty!

BODY MASS
2/10

SKULL SIZE
6/10

FIGHTING SKILLS
8/10

SPEED
7/10

EXISTED FOR
5/10

= TOTAL SCORE

28/50

ANDREWSARCHUS

Andrewsarchus is the largest meat-eating land **mammal** so far discovered. It looked like a cross between a tiger and a wolf, but it was neither a cat nor a dog – it was most closely related to the toothed whales. Andrewsarchus lived in Asia near to lakes and rivers, and the first **fossils** were discovered in Mongolia by palaeontologist Kan Chuen Pao.

BODY MASS

It was a lot bigger than a polar bear. Andrewsarchus measured 5 metres in length (excluding the tail), and weighed about 1,000 kilograms.

SKULL SIZE

Andrewsarchus had a massive skull about 100 centimetres in length.

FIGHTING SKILLS

Andrewsarchus was not a very efficient hunter, and if it ate large animals they were probably **carrion**. It mainly hunted turtles and other small animals that it found near riverbanks.

Powerful jaws and strong teeth could easily crush turtle shells.

SPEED

Andrewsarchus was not built for long chases, and it most likely relied on stealth to take its **prey** by surprise.

This predator probably had spotted fur for camouflage.

EXISTED FOR

Andrewsarchus lived during the late **Eocene** period, about 42-37 million years ago.

The biggest-ever meat-eating mammal – Andrewsarchus was larger than a family car and had sharper teeth.

BODY MASS
4/10

SKULL SIZE
7/10

FIGHTING SKILLS
8/10

SPEED
3/10

EXISTED FOR
7/10

= TOTAL SCORE

The chalicotheres are one of the most puzzling groups of ancient beasts. They lived during the **Eocene** period, and were widespread in Asia, Europe, North Africa and North America. Chalicotheres had forelegs that were much longer than their hind legs, and strange elongated heads – their nearest living relatives are horses.

BODY MASS

Most chalicotheres ranged in size from goat to gorilla – the largest stood about 3 metres tall.

SKULL SIZE

The large, elongated skull is the chalicothere's most horse-like feature. The **jaws** had chewing teeth at the back, but no front teeth.

FIGHTING SKILLS

The long front legs gave it a good reach, but the claws were designed for digging up roots or dragging down branches, and were not much use in a fight.

This jaw bone found in agate fossil beds near Nebraska, United States.

Large, ugly and probably very smelly, chalicotheres would not make a good dancing partners.

SPEED

Chalicotheres were bulky, clumsy beasts that probably tried to climb trees to escape from danger rather than run away.

EXISTED FOR

Chalicothere lived during the whole of the **Eocene** from 53–37 million years ago.

Some species walked on the knuckles of their forefeet, rather than on the soles.

BODY MASS 5/10

SKULL SIZE 7/10

FIGHTING SKILLS 4/10

SPEED 4/10

EXISTED FOR 10/10

= TOTAL SCORE 30/50

AMBULOCETUS

Ambulocetus was a medium-sized **predator** that was equally at home in water or on land. This meat-eating **mammal** could tackle **prey** much larger than its own size. Ambulocetus lived in Asia and Africa about 50 million years ago. The first **fossils** of Ambulocetus were discovered in Pakistan.

BODY MASS
It had a total length of about 3 metres, including the tail, and weighed about 300 kilograms.

SKULL SIZE
Ambulocetus was one of the earliest whales, and it had an elongated skull with rows of sharp teeth.

FIGHTING SKILLS
Its legs were fairly weak and its claws useless for fighting, but its powerful **jaws** and sharp teeth were a fearsome weapon.

Ambulocetus may have dragged its prey below the surface to drown.

Its overall shape was rather like a crocodile.

SPEED

It was fairly slow on land, but faster in the water, where it could use its feet as paddles.

EXISTED FOR

Ambulocetus lived during the early part of the **Eocene** period, about 58-40 million years ago

Its name means "walking whale" – it was a killer whale with four legs.

BODY MASS
6/10

SKULL SIZE
7/10

FIGHTING SKILLS
6/10

SPEED
9/10

EXISTED FOR
5/10

= TOTAL SCORE
33/50

Indricothere is the largest land **mammal** that has ever lived on Earth. This giant **herbivore** once lived in southern Asia. It was taller than a present-day giraffe, and was much more heavily built. Despite its long-necked appearance, the nearest living relative of Indricothere is the rhinoceros.

BODY MASS

Indricothere stood up to 8 metres tall and weighed more than 15,000 kilograms. They were bigger than the largest members of the elephant family, but not as large as whales.

SKULL SIZE

Compared with the rest of its body, Indricotherium's skull was small and lightweight. The male would have had a larger and more domed skull than the female.

FIGHTING SKILLS

Its great size was probably its best defence, and even a **predator** such as Andrewsarchus would have been wary of a kick from one of its massive feet.

Indricotheres probably lived in family groups like elephants do today.

SPEED

Indricotheres ate leaves from branches high above the ground so it had no need to move quickly to catch **prey**. Its bulk meant it faced few predators.

EXISTED FOR

This massive mammal lived during the **Oligocene** period, about 35 million years ago.

Indricotherium is the largest mammal that ever walked the Earth.

If you ventured too close, you would be in danger of being trodden flat by this immense mammal.

BODY MASS
10/10

SKULL SIZE
8/10

FIGHTING SKILLS
6/10

SPEED
3/10

EXISTED FOR
7/10

= TOTAL SCORE

MAMMOTHS

Mammoths were shaggy, fur-covered relatives of the elephant that lived during the **Ice Age**. There were several species of large mammoths that lived in Europe, Asia and North America, and some of them had very long **tusks**. There were also dwarf mammoths living on islands near the coast of **California**.

BODY MASS

The Columbian mammoth of North America was one of the largest species and measured more than 4 metres tall. A fully-grown adult weighed about 10,000 kilograms.

All mammoths had a hump behind the head like present-day Asian elephants.

SKULL SIZE

The skull was large and strongly built to provide a firm anchorage for the huge ivory tusks. The chewing teeth were also very large.

The massive chewing teeth had surfaces designed for grinding up vegetation.

FIGHTING SKILL

The tusks were the main weapon and were used for fighting other mammoths as well as for defence against **predators**.

SPEED

Like modern elephants, mammoths could run quite quickly when they wanted to.

EXISTED FOR

Mammoths lived during the **Pliocene** Ice Age, and only became extinct about 15,000 years ago.

If this hairy beast did not spear you with its tusks, it would trample you underfoot.

BODY MASS
9/10

SKULL SIZE
10/10

FIGHTING SKILLS
6/10

SPEED
5/10

EXISTED FOR
5/10

= TOTAL SCORE
35/50

PHORUSRHACOS

Phorusrhacos was one of the biggest and fiercest birds that ever walked the Earth. It was a deadly **predator**, and is sometimes known as the "terror bird". Phorusrhacos could attack and eat **prey** that were as large as a camel. It lived in **South America** about 20 million years ago.

BODY MASS

Phorusrhacos stood about 2.5 metres tall and was heavy for a bird, much too heavy to fly – it weighed up to 150 kilograms.

FIGHTING SKILLS

Its beak was strong enough to snap the spine of an animal the size of a wolf, and it would attack much larger prey.

SKULL SIZE

The skull of Phorusrhacos was about 65 centimetres long, and more than half of this consisted of the deadly curving beak.

Like many of the early birds, Phorusrhacos had claws on its wings as well as its feet.

The strong skull and powerful beak of a dedicated predator.

At the time Phorusrhacos was the fastest thing on two legs, and few animals could escape its deadly beak.

SPEED

Phorusrhacos had tiny wings and could not fly, but it was a fast runner that could outrun most of its prey. It was also strong enough to chase prey over long distances.

EXISTED FOR

Phorusrhacos lived during the **Miocene** period, about 20 million years ago.

BODY MASS
5/10

SKULL SIZE
7/10

FIGHTING SKILLS
6/10

SPEED
10/10

EXISTED FOR
9/10

= TOTAL SCORE
37/50

Imagine a ferocious and wild giant pig with powerful jaws and long, pointed teeth – that is Entelodon, our overall winner. Entelodon was neither a **carnivore** nor a **herbivore**; it was an **omnivore** that ate anything that came along. Its **jaws** were so powerful that it could crunch up the skulls of other animals.

BODY MASS

Entelodon was about the size of a buffalo. It weighed more than 1,000 kilograms.

SKULL SIZE

The skull was massive, and the **jaws** were long and wide with lots of large teeth.

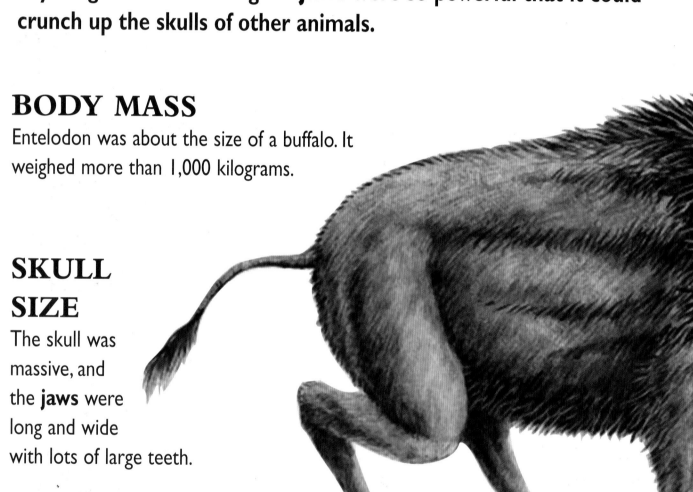

FIGHTING SKILLS

Fossil skulls are often found with terrible wounds. They suggest that Entelodons may have fought among themselves.

These massive jaws could snap a leg as easily as breaking a twig.

Large, powerful, and highly unpredictable – Entelodon was one of the most dangerous beasts of all time.

BODY MASS

7/10

SKULL SIZE

9/10

FIGHTING SKILLS

10/10

SPEED

7/10

EXISTED FOR

8/10

= TOTAL SCORE

SPEED

Entelodon was a fast runner, but it mainly used its speed to escape from danger, and did not chase after its **prey**.

EXISTED FOR

Entelodon lived in North America during the **Oligocene** period, about 35-25 million years ago.

This giant relative of pigs would eat anything it could find.

Choosing just ten ancient beasts for this book was very difficult. Here are five beasts that didn't quite make the final list...

DESMOSTYLIANS

The desmostylians were a very strange group of **mammals** that lived about 35 million years ago. They were about the same size as present-day horses, and lived in shallow water along coastlines. They may have walked along the seabed, while using their peculiar teeth to dig out shellfish. The desmostylians were not closely related to any of the mammals that exist today.

MEGATHERIUM

Megatherium was a gigantic, shaggy-haired ground sloth that only became extinct about 10,000 years ago. This mammal lived in South America, and grew to more than 6 metres in length. Megatherium was a **herbivore** that fed mainly on the leaves and shoots of trees. It walked on all fours, but could stand up on its hind legs to reach the higher branches. It was hunted by sabre-toothed cats.

ARSINOITHERIUM

Arsinoitherium was a horned mammal that lived in Africa about 35 million years ago. Despite its appearance, it was not related to the present-day rhinoceros. The twin horns of Arsinoitherium were made of bone and were a part of the animal's skull. The horn of a rhinoceros, however, is not part of the skull and it is made from tightly compressed hair.

STEGODON

Stegodon lived in Africa and Asia about 10-12 million years ago. It was related to mammoths and present-day elephants, and had the same long trunk, but its tusks tended to be longer and much straighter. The longest **fossil** Stegodon **tusks** that have so far been discovered were each more than 3 metres in length.

BULLOCKORNIS

Bullockornis was a giant duck that lived in Australia about 20 million years ago. It had long, powerful legs and stood about 3 metres tall. Although Bullockornis was a kind of duck, it did not have a flat duck's bill. Instead, it had a large, curved beak that was most likely used to tear strips of flesh from the carcasses of dead animals.

NO. 10 GASTORNIS

Animal type:	Bird	Extreme Scores		
Fossil location:	Europe	Body Mass		3
Food:	Carnivore	Skull Size		5
Living relatives:	Hoatzin	Fighting Skills		6
Discovered by:	Gaston Planté	Speed		6
Main feature:	Enormous beak	Existed for		6

TOTAL SCORE **26 / 50**

NO. 9 MACRAUCHENIA

Animal type:	Mammal	Extreme Scores		
Fossil location:	South America	Body Mass		8
Food:	Herbivore	Skull Size		4
Living relatives:	none	Fighting Skills		2
Discovered by:	Charles Darwin	Speed		8
Main feature:	Running speed	Existed for		5

TOTAL SCORE **27 / 50**

NO. 8 SABRE-TOOTHED CATS

Animal type:	Mammal	Extreme Scores		
Fossil location:	Africa, North America	Body Mass		2
Food:	Carnivore	Skull Size		6
Living relatives:	Tiger	Fighting Skills		8
Discovered by:	L Anderson	Speed		7
Main feature:	Dagger-like teeth	Existed for		5

TOTAL SCORE **28 / 50**

NO. 7 ANDREWSARCHUS

Animal type:	Mammal	Extreme Scores		
Fossil location:	Asia	Body Mass		4
Food:	Carnivore	Skull Size		7
Living relatives:	Killer Whale	Fighting Skills		8
Discovered by:	Kan Chuen Pao	Speed		3
Main feature:	Massive skull	Existed for		7

TOTAL SCORE **29 / 50**

NO. 6 CHALICOTHERES

Animal type:	Mammal	Extreme Scores		
Fossil location:	Europe, Asia, Africa, North America	Body Mass		5
		Skull Size		7
Food:	Herbivore	Fighting Skills		4
Living relatives:	Horses	Speed		4
Discovered by:	Forsyth Major	Existed for		10
Main feature:	Long front legs			

TOTAL SCORE **30 / 50**

NO. 5 AMBULOCETUS

Animal type:	*Mammal*	**Extreme Scores**	**TOTAL SCORE**
Fossil location:	*Asia, Africa*	**Body Mass**	6
Food:	*Carnivore*	**Skull Size**	7
Living relatives:	*Killer Whale*	**Fighting Skills**	6
Discovered by:	*Hans Thewissen*	**Speed**	9
Main feature:	*Powerful jaws*	**Existed for**	5

33 / 50

NO. 4 INDRICOTHERIUM

Animal type:	*Mammal*	**Extreme Scores**	**TOTAL SCORE**
Fossil location:	*Asia*	**Body Mass**	10
Food:	*Herbivore*	**Skull Size**	8
Living relatives:	*Rhinoceros*	**Fighting Skills**	6
Discovered by:	*C. Forster Cooper*	**Speed**	3
Main feature:	*Great size*	**Existed for**	7

34 / 50

NO. 3 MAMMOTH

Animal type:	*Mammal*	**Extreme Scores**	**TOTAL SCORE**
Fossil location:	*North America*	**Body Mass**	9
Food:	*Herbivore*	**Skull Size**	10
Living relatives:	*Asian Elephants*	**Fighting Skills**	6
Discovered by:	*Unknown*	**Speed**	5
Main feature:	*Ivory tusks*	**Existed for**	5

35 / 50

NO. 2 PHORSRHACOS

Animal type:	*Bird*	**Extreme Scores**	**TOTAL SCORE**
Fossil location:	*South America*	**Body Mass**	5
Food:	*Carnivore*	**Skull Size**	7
Living relatives:	*Parrots*	**Fighting Skills**	6
Discovered by:	*Benjamin Waller*	**Speed**	10
Main feature:	*Powerful beak*	**Existed for**	9

37 / 50

NO. 1 ENTELODON

Animal type:	*Mammal*	**Extreme Scores**	**TOTAL SCORE**
Fossil location:	*North America*	**Body Mass**	7
Food:	*Omivore*	**Skull Size**	9
Living relatives:	*Wild pigs*	**Fighting Skills**	10
Discovered by:	*Gaston Plante*	**Speed**	7
Main feature:	*Bone-crunching jaws*	**Existed for**	8

41 / 50

CARNIVORE a meat-eating animal

CARRION the dead and rotting body of an animal

EOCENE a period of history from 58 million to 40 million years ago when the first modern mammals appeared

EPOCH a unit or period of geologic time

FOSSIL the remains of an animal that has turned to stone

HERBIVORE a plant-eating animal

ICE AGE any period of time during which glaciers covered a large part of the earth's surface. The most recent occurred from 2 million to 11 thousand years ago

JAWS the structures that form the framework of the mouth

JOINT a point of the body that enables two bones to move

MAMMAL any of various warm-blooded animals with a covering of hair on the skin and, in the female, the ability to produce milk with which to feed the young.

MIOCENE a period of time from 25 million to 13 million years ago, that saw the appearance of grazing mammals

OLIGOCENE a period of time from 40 million to 25 million years ago, that saw the appearance of sabre-toothed cats

OMNIVORE an animal that eats both meat and plants

PALAEONTOLOGIST a scientist who specialises in the study of fossil organisms and related remains

PREDATOR an animal that lives by preying on other animals

PREY an animal hunted or caught for food

PLIOCENE the last epoch of the Tertiary period that saw the appearance of modern looking animals

QUATERNARY period of time covering the last 2 million years

SPINE series of vertebrae forming the axis of the skeleton and protecting the spinal cord

TERTIARY period of time from 63 million to 2 million years ago, that saw the appearance of modern flora, apes and other large mammals

TUSK a long pointed tooth specialized for fighting or digging; especially in an elephant or walrus